LEVEL UP

How your Gaming,
and your walk
with God collide

CHERYL ANDERSEN

WESTBOW
PRESS®
A DIVISION OF THOMAS NELSON
& ZONDERVAN

WestBow Press books may be ordered through booksellers or by contacting:

WestBow Press
A Division of Thomas Nelson & Zondervan
1663 Liberty Drive
Bloomington, IN 47403
www.westbowpress.com
844-714-3454

ISBN: 978-1-6642-4158-9 (sc)
ISBN: 978-1-6642-4159-6 (e)

Library of Congress Control Number: 2021915258

Print information available on the last page.

WestBow Press rev. date: 09/09/2021

ACKNOWLEDGMENTS

First, I give credit to my God. The very same God who rescued me from a life I chose when I took the wrong path. He psalms 40:1-3 picked me up, set my feet back on solid ground. He is my Guide, my scout, my deliverer, and my strength! Without him, I would be stuck in the wrong path.

My God of second chances.

Second, would like to thank my mom. (Millie Ayres) She stood by me, and never gave up on me. She always spoke life into me. She spoke of the power of our choices. And how it was the greatest power we possess. Later, I found the scripture to back that truth.

I also would like to say thank you to: Patricia Broadwater for your illustration to my book. I appreciate you so much.

ABOUT THIS INTERACTIVE BOOK

This Bible study/Book may be gone through cover to cover, just like any other study, or book. However, I encourage you to explore the optional interactive elements for a more personalized experience.

See yourself in life's battles, know what weapons are available to you in Christ. Know the power of your choices either move you forward, or keep you from advancing.

Knowing God fights for you is as important, as knowing the enemy.

I pray you get to know your superpower, who fights for you, goes ahead you. That you find the strengths of your weapons.

And learn how to: **Level Up**!

LEADER SUMMARY

Offer a sign-up sheet to find out how many youths will be attending so, you know how many books to order before you begin your study.

Also, I have listed songs I am particularly fond of, but you can choose your own. Pick at least two songs to play before you begin each session, and one or two songs to end each session.

May God move in the hearts of our youth, as they grow and learn how effective it is to know God's truth and the weapons that are available to them, to, level up!

Level Up!

Leaders, *start by playing a few worship songs. If you have a player and are licensed to use and show music videos, these are great ones:*

- *Ryan Stevenson: "Amadeo (Still My God)"*
- *Vertical Worship: "Faithful Now".*
- *Hillsong "Young and Free: Best Friends" (Live Version)*

Good _____ (morning, afternoon, evening), I will be talking about something I am sure most of you can relate to.

How many gamers do we have in the room? How many are beginners? And how many have never gamed? Well, don't worry if you are a solid gamer, or a beginner, maybe you have never gamed. You can apply these strategies and techniques to your life.

So, is it safe to say you understand strategy, skill, and what it takes to level up? Can someone give me a rundown of how you start, and what it takes to get to the next level?

(Pause for answer.)

It is my understanding that the challenge is to learn all the strategies that you can, gaining skills and understanding during level 1, right? Learning the strengths and weaknesses of your opponent, or enemy, is probably a great tool, too. In some games you gain weapons for further battles, correct? And, once, you have level down, and have grown stronger in knowledge, strength, and wisdom, what is next? Do you level up? At each new level what keeps you intrigued, and what keeps you striving over and over again? Isn't it safe to say the goal is to reach the next level?

Well, it is just like that in our walk with God. In the beginning, we accept the first part of the challenge: repentance and asking and accepting God into our lives and hearts. How about spending time with God in prayer and his word? When we spend time doing these things, we get to know God, and establish a relationship with him. Here we begin to see how he operates in our lives.

In a game, knowing who goes with you and fights for you is important to your strength as well. Isn't that, right? I know that in a game you can even have scouts who go before you to look for obstacles or land mines so to speak.

God also is a great scout, as he goes before us to prepare the way, looking for traps the enemy has set for our distraction, demise and destruction.

> It is the Lord who goes before you. He will
> be with you; he will not leave you
> or forsake you. Do not fear or be
> dismayed." (Deuteronomy 31:8 ESV)

> I will go before you and make the rough places
> smooth. I will shatter the doors of bronze and
> cut through iron bars. (Isaiah 45:2NASB)

> I can almost see the picture of God going before
> you, smashing down any obstacle in your way.
> Nothing is so fierce that God cannot conquer it.)

> And the Lord was going before them in a
> pillar of cloud by day to lead them
> on the way, and a pillar of fire by night
> to give them light, that they might
> travel by day, and by night. (Exodus 13:21 NASB)

> The angel of God, who had been going
> before the camp of Israel, moved and
> went behind them. And the pillar of
> cloud moved before them and stood
> behind them. (Exodus 14:14:19 NASB)

Wow! I love these scriptures because they show God setting up a hedge of protection! Is it just me, or can you relate these scriptures to tactics in a game?

Below are additional scriptures that give more clarity, and insight, into what it looks like to walk with God—who also is a great scout, and protector.

> Who goes before you on your way, to seek
> out a place for you to make camp,
> in fire by night to show you the way by
> which you should go, and in the cloud
> by day. (Deuteronomy 1:33 NASB)

This is a perfect visual of a scout. Let us look at a few more tactics that are useful.

When you begin a game is there a manual, or instructions that help you to know the game and its contents?

God's word the Bible contains your basic instructions for life.

B—Basic
I—Instructions
B—Before
L—Leaving
E—Earth

In his word, God provided us everything we need to know to spend eternity with him. Let us look at, 2 Timothy 3:16-17 (NIV).

> All scripture is God breathed and is useful
> for teaching, rebuking, correcting,
> and training in righteousness, so that the
> servant of God may be thoroughly
> equipped for every good work.

This scripture tells you the superpowers of your user's manual, - the Bible. Knowing I have weapons at my disposal to take on the challenges and defeat the enemy is key to winning. Don't you agree? It gives you guidelines in how to act, and it is a clear and easy set of rules we can apply to our lives to help us deal with tough situations and people.

Choice is the key, and obedience is the action. These seems to be the key you carry through the whole game.

Let us look a little bit deeper into scripture to see what additional powerful knowledge God gives to us:

> Put on the whole armor of God, that you may stand firm against the schemes of the devil.

> For our struggle is not against flesh and blood, but against the rulers, against the powers against the world-forces of this darkness, against the spiritual forces of wickedness in the heavenly places Therefore take up the full armor of God, so that you will be able to resist on the evil day, and, having done everything to stand firm. (Ephesians 6:11-13 NASB)

In your games is there ever a time you must suit up, so you can effectively fight your enemy? Who are your enemies in real life? Are they the bullies down the street?

The drug dealers on the corner? Those people who are always tearing you down, and belittling you?

What strategy do you use when dealing with them? And are there times when you have armor, or shields, swords, and weapons available to you for battle?

Did you know that your Bible gives you the very same things? (Cool, right?)

Let us continue in Ephesians 6:14-17 (NIV)

> Stand firm then, with the belt of truth buckled around your waist, with the breastplate of righteousness in place, and with your feet fitted with the readiness that comes with the gospel of peace. In addition to all this, take up the shield of faith, (which believes in all things and hopes in all things) with which you can extinguish all the flaming arrows of the evil one. Take the helmet of salvation and the sword of Spirit, which is the word of God.

Your armor is God's protection—as we have learned, the enemy has forces all his own.

We will start with the helmet of salvation. Does the enemy attack us in our thoughts?

Absolutely! Does he whisper lies telling us we're not good enough, and we will never be worthy? Of course, he is a liar! So, is the helmet of salvation a form of protection against things like that? You know it is!

And knowing who you are in Christ is a weapon you can always throw back at him.

We'll move on to the breastplate of righteousness—Does it protect the warrior's vital organs? Is not the heart especially important, not only in your body but in God's word?

"For the heart (the understanding of the soul) of this people has become dull(calloused)

> and with their ears they scarcely hear, and
> they have shut their eyes, [to the truth,
> otherwise, they might see with their eyes,
> and hear with their ears, and understand

with their heart and return [to me] and I would heal them."
(Acts 28:27AMP)

What happens to us when our hearts are hardened from circumstances or bitterness? It is hard to see with eyes of love, it is hard to hear with open minds, and anger and rebelliousness entangles the heart. So, the breastplate covers an especially important vital organ both to you and God.

Create in me a pure heart, O God, and renew a steadfast spirit within me.
(Psalm 51:10 NIV)

What about the belt of truth? It's a weapon all its own. I googled "belt of truth," and this is what I found:

Vital to every soldier was this belt from which all the tools of battle hung. This belt also held the soldier's robe together. To the Christian soldier a belt of truth means "honesty", "truthfulness," "integrity" and "sincerity" that surrounds every part of life!

Oh wow! How powerful is that! I think it is safe to say that truth, and the morality of it, is your weapon!

Let us take your shield of faith:

Your shield of faith that believes in all things, and hopes all things are true. When the enemy, your opponent comes at you with lies, and fear, you can block those darts with your shield of faith.

> Now faith is the substance of things hoped
> for, the evidence of things not yet seen.
> Though at times we do not see the power
> of God at work, knowing he is working in
> the unseen is powerful walking- as though
> he is working is faith!
> (Hebrews 11:1 KJV)

(A simple prayer: God, though I do not see the evidence yet of my prayer, I know you are at work.)

Let us move on to your sword of the Spirit.

The sword of the Spirit is a particularly important part of the armor of God, it is to be used both offensively and defensively by Christians.

The word- *offensively-* is used as: "fighting a war or battle aggressively"—to advance against an army.

The word *defensively* is used as: "in a manner intended to defend or protect. Jesus used scripture defensively against the enemy during the temptation in the wilderness.

You can call upon your sword for whatever battle you are facing. Remember we do not fight battles with flesh, and blood, but against the devil and his forces. Let's say the devil is coming against you by causing fear and anxiety. Use your sword of the Spirit to attack those things specifically.

Let me give you a scripture to clarify the power of what you call upon.

> "Truly I tell you, whatever you bind on earth will be bound in heaven, and whatever you loose on earth will be loosed in heaven."
> (Mathew 18:18 NIV)

Your armor backed by what you call upon in truth is powerful!

Ok, we have reached the shoes/boots of peace. Having our feet fitted with the shoes of the gospel of peace allows us to be ready to always share God with others.

As Christians we should always be prepared, as we never know when an opportunity may arise to share the gospel with someone.

I don't know how you see it, but walking with God is a mirror of playing your game. At this point, you have knowledge, are fully equipped, and are ready to go to the next level, or step, in your walk with God.

You have accepted God into your hearts and are growing in his word, you have weapons, and armor, and you know your strength. You have opened a line of communication, and you're seeing God move in your life. Because you are in a relationship with God's character, you know he is trustworthy. You can rely on him, and his word.

What is the next step in this level with God?

You will come to a place of Baptism. It is part of level 1 and is a particularly important step. It is here that you let go of the old person, the old character, and are reborn and equipped with the Holy Spirit. The Holy Spirit is the third person of the trinity: (Father, Son, and Holy Spirit.) The Holy Spirit is your helper/guide, and he can lead, guide, and direct you. Also, the Holy Spirit speaks on your behalf to the Father.

> Then Peter said unto them, "Repent and be baptized every one of you in the name of Jesus. Christ for the remission of sins. And ye will receive the Holy ghost."
> (Acts 2:38 KJV)

> Jesus answered, "Very truly I tell you, no one can enter the kingdom of God unless they are born of water and Spirit." (John 3:5 NIV)

Do these look-like clues to get to the next level?

What if- I told you an especially important key, clue, or weapon to carry with you? What if-

I told you it holds the power over life and death? And what if I told you, it is "the greatest power we possess?"

Would you take it with you to call upon when you are in difficult places?

This weapon and tool is: The power of choice! You cannot move to any other level without making the right choices. You begin with it, and end with it! You choose to believe that Jesus is the son of God and, that he gave his life for us, so we could have a relationship with him.

Knowing that it was that sacrifice that set us free and offered us forgiveness of sins gives us freedom in Him and allows us to move forward. You choose freely to be baptized, and you are given Life and a Helper, the Holy Spirit.

Level 1 is completed!

LEVEL 2

> This day I call the heavens and the earth as witness against you that I have set before you life and death, blessings and curses. Now choose life, so that you and your children may live."
>
> (Deuteronomy 30:19 NIV)

Again, this scripture tells you of how great the power of choice is. You literally hold the key to your outcome. Isn't it the same in your game?

Things begin to change, as you go through levels. Each level is activated by a new choice. Until you choose to take the next step, you stay in that place, on that level.

In your games you are only given so many lives. What happens when you die? Do you begin again? And go until what? Until you learn what it takes to avoid the land mines and the things that took you out the first time.

It's like that in your walk with God. Grace finds you, and with a repentant and eager heart you can begin again. It is always just one step back into grace and repentance with a sincere heart.

What are some obstacles in real life that can cause major setbacks?

- drugs
- alcohol
- crime
- hanging with wrong people

(Allow participants to give any additional)

Let's remember these obstacles. We will discuss them a little later.

Whatever setbacks or challenges you may face, it is how you choose to go through them, and who you choose to navigate them with that will determine how you come out. Choosing to go it alone, in your own strength you may not come out so well. Your life tends to become drained when lived in its own strength. Or you may keep repeating the same patterns, until you finally choose right. But, if you choose to go through with God as your scout, strength, and wisdom you are going to get to the other side of through.... Well!

Let us look at 2 Corinthians 12:9 (NIV).

> But he said to me, "My grace is sufficient for you, for my power is made perfect in weakness." Therefore, I will boast all the more gladly about my weakness, so that Christ's power may rest in me.

This is a picture of what that looks like: Though you are weak, God's strength is sufficient to carry you through as you rely on him. How many times do we go through difficult times on our own, trying to figure it out, and find all the right answers to help us get out of a situation.

only to be left frustrated and clueless as to what the key is to get out of it? But, in the moment of surrendering the life problem to God, we cry out "God, I need you! This is too difficult for me on my own!" At this very moment, God is activated to step in.

But God cannot operate until you give him authority. God knows as long as you are determined to do it on your own that there is no place for him. Therefore, when you give it to him in trust, he becomes the power over your weakness. I do not know about you, but that is one of my greatest truths that I stand on often!

So, if things are not working out, ask yourself, "Who's will am I operating in mine or God's?" At each challenge, there is a choice.

Remember, in the beginning of this lesson I told you that you have a superpower?

It is the greatest power we possess because everything we do in life revolves around choice! Get up out of bed or don't, decide what outfit to wear, decide what food to eat, and even decide what words to speak, and in what manner we speak them. So, if you chose God as your scout and strength, you've made the right choice. You are moving on.

Let us look at Deuteronomy 30:19 (NIV), where it says,

> "I have set before you life and
> death, blessings and curses".

Imagine if you will, you are at a point in the game where you come to a Y in the road. To the right is an entrance and above it, are the words: choose Life. The other path to the left says: choose your own way. *Do you see the choice?*

Player 1 chooses the path to the right. It is the good path and well lit. God walks this path with him as his overseer and protector. He comes up against challenges, and hardships along the way.

But God is with him, and Holy Spirit wisdom is guiding him. He still must face the trials. But the trials he faces with God are strengthening him, growing him strong, and giving him courage.

Each trial or temptation that he overcomes with God's help is *empowering* him for future levels.

Now let us look at player 2. He also stands at the Y. In a moment of weakness, he hears a voice calling him to take the "Choose your own way" path. The voice tempts him with his own desire. It is fun here. Choose this way, and he does.

As the player peers down the path, the deceiver has dressed it up to look inviting, adventurous, enticing, a little risky, and with some danger mixed in.

Player 2 chooses this way, this way that does not lead to life, or blessings, only curses and death are found here.

As he enters, the player chooses to enter in here alone and unprotected, God cannot enter with him. This does not mean God does not love him or has abandoned him. He cannot enter this path of sin. He can watch over you and will even protect you, but his hands are tied. When you operate in your own will, it renders his will useless.

Patiently, your loving Father is waiting for you to surrender, repent, and come back to the place you left him when you entered down the wrong path.

Now let us discuss the three bad choices that can lead you down that path of destruction and distraction. But before we do, let's look at the meaning of these two words:

- Distraction: A thing that prevents someone from giving full attention to something else!
- Destruction: The action or process of causing so much damage to something it can no longer exist or be repaired although, we know God is the restorer, even after we mess up.

Remember a little bit earlier in the session, when, I asked you to come up with some obstacles of distraction that derail us in our walk? Some of the big ones are drugs, alcohol, bad influences, and crime. Feel free to add anything else you may come up with.

So, what happens when you take this path of destruction?

In that place, there can be heavy consequences, and major setbacks. Addiction, loss, jails, institutions, and death - and death is not always physical. It's the death of hopes, and dreams, it's the death of time, time you cannot get back.

It's the death of relationships, and trust. Trust, once lost, is hard to get back!

You lose your dignity, and your self-respect, and your life levels are low: low self-worth, low

self-esteem, low trust. You find yourself in a pattern of low, repeating itself in all the wrong ways.

In this level, you get stuck!

Depending on how long it takes you to realize this was the wrong choice, the wrong path, determines how long you stay in this holding pattern. Years could have passed like days. Some will not make it out sadly. I know some of you already know this disheartening truth- and what it feels like to have a friend, or family member struggle, and even lose their life in this battle. I know I have! And it's heart breaking! If I could use an emoji, it would be a heart broken in half or a crying face! This path is unforgiving, cruel, and without mercy! Do not despair. There is a way out, but it depends on you, because only you hold the key.

God tied his own hands by giving us free will. He will not do anything until you surrender.

Think of the scripture quoted above, 2 Corinthians 12:9 (NIV).

This is where his strength is made perfect when we choose to call upon him to help. The choice is the key to getting back to the good place. Making the right choice can get you back to the place of Y. Choosing to cry out to a loving God who has waited for you to choose him in repentance and forgiveness is your life power.

> I waited patiently for the Lord; he turned
> to me and heard my cry. He lifted me out
> of the slimy pit, out of the mud and mire;
> he set my feet on a rock and gave me a
> firm place to stand. He put a new song in
> my mouth, a hymn of praise to our God.
> Many will see an fear the Lord and put
> their trust in him.
> (Psalm 40:1-3)

God will rescue you! It is important to know that!

(A simple prayer: God, you know who I am, and you know all the things I have done. There is nothing I am hiding from you. Please forgive me, I cannot do this without you! Give me strength, and help me out of this place. In Jesus's name, amen.)

Level up

Now that we see what happened to the player who chose the wrong path, let us journey back to the level where the two players stood at a Y in the road. Each had a choice as to which road to take. Each path, each choice had a destination attached to it. We see the player who took his own way, down the wrong road.

The player who chose to go right chose the road that continued to lead to Life. He's moved forward, gaining strength and blessings. God is using him in his church and community. God has equipped him with strength and wisdom. Many battles they have gone through together in victory!

Remember your truths: 2 Corinthians 12:8-10— Say's to - know where your strength comes from.

Ephesians 6:10-18 (NIV). Don't forget about your Armor of protection! These are the truths that Player 1 walked in. They sustained him through the battles.

There is another truth you must know. Just because God walks with this player fights for him, a is his strength, hope, and life, there still will be tough battles, rocky roads, and the loss of people in his life. There will be times when the storms of life hit and sometimes in epic proportions. They can have you questioning everything.

Why, God? Why?

Don't lose heart. Stand strong in this place, and keep your eyes on the one who controls the waves! The Master of the tempest!

Let us look at John 16:33 (NIV).

> I have told you these things, so, that in me you may
> have peace. In this world you will have trouble,
> but take heart! I have overcome the world."

God doesn't want us to be powerless. It is the hard times, the tough times, that strengthen our character, and grow our faith as we look to God to show us the way. Our relationship with him, - getting into God's word, - and knowing his promises will get you through.

Here is another powerful scripture to mark:

> Trust in the Lord, with all your heart! Do
> not lean on your own understanding, in all
> your ways acknowledge him, and he will
> direct your path.
> (Proverbs 3:5-6 NKJV).

He is your trusted Guide.

Let me ask a question. When you are on a level, - and have been there for a while, do you give up, or are you challenged to try harder, seeking new ways to navigate? What happens in this place? Are your skills being sharpened? Do you gain new wisdom, learning more about the tools and weapons at your disposal? And how about learning about the tactics of your enemy so you can defeat him? Life is so much like this.

I hope that you take and apply these lessons to your life!

Can someone tell me what the one word found in Deuteronomy 30:19 (NIV) and found throughout every move, every step, and every new level is?

Choice is the greatest power you possess!

> This day I call the heavens and earth
> as witnesses against you that I have set
> before your life and death, blessing and
> curses. Now <u>choose</u> life, so that you and
> your children may live, and that you may
> love the Lord your God, listen to his voice,
> and hold fast to him. For the Lord is your
> life, and he will give you many years in
> the land he swore to give to your fathers,
> Abraham, Isaac and Jacob. (Deuteronomy
> 30:19-20 NIV)

Everything we do in life revolves around our choices! Each choice has a consequence and a destination attached to it. Carry it with you... play each choice to the end result! "What and where will this choice take me, what are the consequences?" Look at the consequences, and the destination of your choices. If it does not produce life, and Blessings, walk (or run) away....

Level Up!

<u>Leaders,</u> pray them out and be available for individual prayer.

I would like to reference a few great songs for closing.

- Matthew West: "The God Who Stays"
- Sean Curran: "All Praise (live from Passion Camp)"

But you should play whatever the Spirit leads you to play.

LEVEL UP!

I want you to see just how your walk with God, and your gaming reflect each other.

It's important to know who goes before you, and who fights for you. Knowing what weapons are available to you as you go through life, and what your superpower is.

God is your scout, your strength, your life power, and weapon!

Knowing your God, and all he has available to you, through his word will help you navigate this thing called life.

Just as it is in your games you play there is strategy, weapons of warfare, tactics.

If you make a wrong move, or choose the wrong path you may begin again.

But one thing determines if you move forward, Choice!

Make the right choices you move on, make the wrong one you stay stuck on your level, or begin again.

The *key* is that you keep moving forward in your walk with God.

And, that you continue to: LEVEL UP!